This is a work of nonfiction. Names, characters, places, and incidents are either the product of the author's personal experiences or imagination. Names have been changed to protect the innocent and those not so innocent, including the author. Any other resemblance other than the authors experiences are entirely coincidental.

Millennial Love Sucks!

But Does it Have to?

ISBN: 978-0-9884734-1-6

First Edition (print): January 2013

To all the hearts I have broken and those who broke

mine. Our stories are not yet over.

C. L. Bartley

Table of Contents

Chapter 1
Introduction

Something is wrong here. Alarming amounts of people living within the Millennial Generation in particular, have no idea what love is. Nor do they know how to obtain, and more importantly, sustain that love. Why is that? I look around and see so many people in relationships, but behind closed doors, it is certainly not filled with rose petals and endless smiles. Not even close! What gives?!

Is it our parents' fault? Is it the Internet? Social media? Society? Hollywood? Aliens? The answer might be a combination of all of the above. Yes, including aliens. Who am I to say they don't exist? However, I am here to say that too long have we pointed fingers at who *else* is to blame. Should we investigate on what or who else is to blame? Perhaps it might be worth exploring at another time, but not today. In my opinion, that will not solve the problems that are before us.

Do me a favor. Go to your nearby restroom; turn on the light, look at the mirror. What do you see? That is who we will be talking about in this book. Ourselves. We need to look within ourselves before we can look at others around us.

You may be asking yourself, "Who is this guy writing a book on relationships and love? Does he have a Ph.D. in

Psychology and years of counseling under his belt?" In short, the answer is, "Nope. I am you." I have, and currently do, live in the dating world. (And what a horrible world it can be.) I am divorced. I have experienced the highs and lows of relationships, just like you. I have felt the excitement of the chase and the crushing defeat of rejection. I have watched best friends enter into a relationship train wreck, warning them exactly how it would turn out, but to no avail. (I was right by the way.) I am the everyday man, who would like to think that maybe I have experienced enough to write a small book. After all, the old saying goes, "Those who can't do, teach."

So what gives me the right to write anything on this subject? Why should you listen to me? My response is... listen or don't listen to me. I do not have a degree in Psychology or Sociology or formal counseling experience. I do, however, have far too many relationships under my belt. To be clear, I am not being boastful. I would rather have one great relationship over hundreds of failed ones, and I am guessing you might feel the same since you are now reading this book. Oh, and to clarify, I am not referring to one-night stands as relationships either. I say again, I am not insinuating that I have had hundreds of one-night stands!

If you are reading this hoping to find the skills to pick someone up at a bar, you probably won't find them. If I knew how to do that each and every night, I wouldn't be sitting in front of this computer screen right now. I would be out doing it!

If you are like me and have failed in all relationships (and unless you are truly happy in a long-term committed relationship, I am talking to you) then let me help explain what I believe is occurring in our dating world. My guess is that you will laugh (probably at the expense of my 'confessions'), and maybe cry, but hopefully walk away feeling better about the dating world in which we live. And perhaps, you will be more equipped in your own personal dating "hell" that you may or may not be in right now.

A few disclosures before we begin: As I mentioned, I am divorced. This means I believed I found the love of my life and made a valiant effort to make it work. To be clear, I blame most of our failures and ultimate demise on myself. I was the man and therefore, I felt responsible to make it successful. I failed. Very simple. Luckily, this book is not *completely* about my marriage so I will not go into too much detail on this. However, I definitely mention my dating experiences from time to time. Ok, I mention them a lot actually; so prepare to enter my world.

Another disclosure: I am not currently in a wonderfully happy relationship. Actually, I am not in one at all. The reasons why may become clear later in this book, but for now, this will have to suffice. Bottom line is that this guy... is single.

Another: Until about a half a year ago, I flat out refused that true love is even possible (at least for our generation). I had been burned so badly and had such a bad taste in mouth over my own failures and shortcomings that I proclaimed the fallacy of love to anyone I met. I did it loudly and obnoxiously at times to be honest. Interestingly enough, no one believed I actually meant what I said, but I stuck to my guns anyway. This is what males do... stick to bad ideas even though we know it's ridiculous. Again, more on this later.

Another disclosure: My parents. We live in a world where over half of marriages end in divorce, including mine. I consider myself incredibly fortunate that my parents are still together and deeply love one another.   At times, it's sickening actually. I can honestly say that if it wasn't for their example, I may actually believe that love and marital bliss do not exist. Their example is the sole reason why I still believe it is possible.   For my generation?   Well, that is up for debate, which we will work through in the following pages.

Another disclosure: I by no means, in no way possible, not even a little bit, pretend to understand the female psyche. If I did understand it, I would be a quadruple billionaire overnight. Unfortunately, for both you and me, I am like every other man and I become lost in women's minds and emotions almost on a daily basis. Scratch that, definitely on a daily basis. At least I recognize the fact that I have no idea what is going on in the female mind, which is more than I can say for many of my male counterparts. Point for me! And yes, we're keeping score… don't pretend you don't keep score in the game of love.

Another disclosure: I have never been a perfect boyfriend, fiancé, or husband. I have cheated and been cheated on. I have lied and been lied too. I have cried and made others cry. Obviously, I am not proud of any of these things. I regret them all, in fact. Yet, these horrible decisions have shaped who I am and how I now understand the dynamics of relationships. We can't change what we did or where we have been. We can only do our best to understand the 'why' of our past and ultimately, the 'where' we are going in our future.

My last disclosure, and this one may turn you off from reading this book, is that I have done zero literary research. I have not looked up relationship "buzzwords" or used any fancy terms. I have read a few books on love in the past (see the fact, "I am divorced"), but I do not quote anything from those books I have read. All of the thoughts, opinions, and words in this book are entirely mine. The stories and examples I use are either mine, or of close friends who do not want to be named.

After my disclosures, I hope you are still reading. If for nothing else, my opinions on this subject should be entertaining. I am a thirty-year-old single male, who is about to give insight into a guy's mind when it comes to relationships. Many friends (women) seek my advice on their relationship drama because I give it to them straight. I tell them exactly what that cryptic text they just received means. I tell them exactly how to respond in order to get the response they desire. When it comes to this part of the relationship, (the playing games portion), I am fairly good. I'm not exactly proud of that. In fact, that plays a part in why I am writing this fun little book. To help us all stop this nonsense.

Again, I do not claim to be in a happily-ever-after relationship. Therefore, I do not claim to know the secrets to a perfect relationship. If you are like me, this is when you look to an older generation and ask for their secrets. Unfortunately, their secrets do not always translate over the generational divide. They are worth listening to, of course, and their examples can show us that true happiness is possible. However, we are a different generation with different values and norms. That fact simply cannot be overlooked.

The Millennials have grown up more spoiled than any other generation before us. Most, if not all, of us cannot even fathom a world without the Internet or a flat screen TV in every room of our apartments. We grew up with information milliseconds away, rather than spending hours at a public library researching a term paper. Our parents have been the most successful in our country's history and we, as Millennials, have reaped the benefits of this.

Our parents' successes and innovations have inadvertently created monsters. They laid the foundation and we have already taken their ideas leaps and bounds further. Chat rooms, MySpace, Facebook, Twitter and Text Messages: as children or adolescents, we grew up with these tools as ways to connect to our peers and the world. They certainly serve a purpose (sort of) but they have helped shape our skewed view of social interactions and relationships.

When is the last time you sat down and wrote a heart-felt letter? I am writing this on a laptop, not a piece of paper. Even e-mails tend to take too long for us. We would rather post a Facebook status or a Tweet for the world to read. (As if we believe the world cares that we just bought a venti caramel macchiato.) On the other hand, if something is more personal, we send a text message. As long as it is 160 characters or less, it is important enough to say. And who among us has not shortened words and changed "to" into a "2" to make a message fit into one text message? To clarify, I am not saying we should all pick up a feather and ink and write a love letter. I am simply saying we have become accustomed to instant communication and gratification. Our patience is gone and if something takes too much work, we deem it not worth the effort and move on.

What I just described, is how many of us now communicate. Besides my older family members, I do not recall the last person I actually spoke to on the phone and had a meaningful conversation with. In fact, I get irritated when someone calls me. I always think, "What is so important? A text is immediate. I would be done reading the text right now and know what you want, rather than staring at my ringing phone, which is still ringing, and I am not going to answer it. And why am I talking out loud to myself?" (Don't act like you haven't done the exact same thing... Well, maybe not the talking out loud to yourself part...)

I have divulged all of this information willingly and without hesitation because I am confident that many of you out there are the same or at least similar to me. We are flawed individuals, with our own back-stories and skeletons in our closets in terms of what we bring to a relationship. And like me, I bet you're sick of it. I bet you are tired of all the crap that seems to come along with our relationships.

When we enter a relationship, we bring with us our talents, as well as our failures. No matter how hard we try, we are incapable of running from our past, even though we attempt to do so in every relationship we enter. Ever wonder why every relationship ends up the same? The answer does not usually lie with our chosen partners, but in us.

The rest of this exploration in love and relationships will explore what we do, and my opinion, on what we should do in relationships. You may agree or disagree with me, but one of my points I will explore is… that is the beauty of relationships: Perhaps our relationship as writer and reader will flourish, or perhaps it will fail miserably. You as the reader have the choice on what to do next. Enter in this relationship and see what happens, read a few more pages and forget me, or stick in for the long haul and see what this guy is about to say. The choice is yours.

Chapter 2
A Sinking Ship

Where to begin our journey together? First, let me introduce you to one of my major philosophies so that I may set the stage for us. I call it, the "snapshot." Each year, month or day is a snapshot in time. As you read this, you have a certain situation you are in at this exact moment. You also have a set of circumstances behind you, as well as a new set of challenges in front of you.

Maybe your relationship situation is that you are in a one-sided relationship? Maybe you just ended a relationship? Maybe someone ended it for you? Maybe you are happily married and are just looking for a laugh by reading this book? Or maybe you got this book on accident, and are now too intrigued to put it down?

Wherever you are in life at this exact moment is your snapshot. Behind us, we have past experiences that define who we are. When someone looks at us, talks to us, tries to "read" us, all they see is our snapshot. Only the here and now. They have no idea what occurred in our lives to morph us into who we are today. All they see is the cover on the book and perhaps a small teaser to entice them to open the book and read more.

Imagine yourself on a beautiful beach. Someone takes a close up picture of you so that only your smiling face and the setting sun is in the picture. Does that tell you the entire story? What color was the sand? How high were the waves behind you? What are you wearing? Who took the picture and how did you get there?

Most of the people we interact with on a daily basis will never get past this snapshot of our here and now. It takes a lot of effort to get to know someone's back-story or where they might want their future to go. Let's be honest, most of the people we interact with don't fall under this category. Which is why the term "snapshot" is perfect.

Each of us is unique in our own way based on the choices we have made and our experiences we have endured. No one, and I mean no one, is exactly like us. Twins may look alike or even act similarly, however, they have different strengths, weaknesses, communication styles, etc. Ultimately, we all are unique individuals no matter how "similar" we think we are.

People often use the term "soul mate" to identify someone who is exactly like them. That might be somewhat true, but not exactly. "Soul mates", whether it's platonic or romantic, have different pasts. It's possible that two people will end up living in the same city, the same building, at the same point in their lives, yet they come from opposite sides of the country. They have different family situations, socio-economic statuses, different jobs, etc. This makes each of us unique and special, no matter how similar our snapshots are at any given time. Our current snapshots might be nearly identical, but it's important to note that it's only our snapshots that are similar. Not our entire collection of life experiences, nor will our futures be exactly the same.

Many of us make the most common mistake of all and attempt to run from our past. We believe that whatever we did or whatever happened to us will simply stay put while we run away. We make ourselves believe it never happened. Maybe we lived in a small town and experienced a miserable relationship failure. So we move to the big city in a different state, hoping to start fresh. Perhaps we even change who we were and turned from shy to outgoing; from timid to outrageous; the quiet guy to the life of the party. Yet, no matter how far we run, it's never far enough. We will explore that more in the next chapter, but it is important to mention here since this can certainly play a part in our current snapshot.

Making life changes certainly has its merits and can distract us from whatever we are running from. We may become happier than we have ever been and start to believe that life will turn out okay. Yet, something deep down still isn't right. Even when we made the right move to start a brand new job, life, move away, etc., there is still something wrong. But why?

To sum up the "snapshot," I want to point out that our snapshot is ever evolving. Therefore, if you are not a huge fan of your current snapshot in time, don't fret too much. Your snapshot can certainly change. In fact, that is the goal of this book; to change our snapshot from unhappy in relationships and with ourselves, to the kind of people that refuse to play games and who choose to be happy. That choice, in turn, will evolve into a relationship we can be proud of.

Now that we have discussed our snapshots and set the stage for our discussion about our current selves, let's dive right in, shall we? Let's discuss how we got to this point. I believe that in every relationship we enter we give up a part of ourselves, no matter how small that part may be. If that relationship fails, we simply lose that part of us for the time being. This leaves a hole, deep inside, that leaves us feeling empty.

Many times, depending on how long and deep our relationship was, we fill that hole with meaningless activities. Things such as over-eating, not eating, alcohol, meaningless sex, gambling... the list goes on and on. We don't always fill that hole with self-destructive behavior, however, when we're honest with ourselves, most of us do. At least for a short time, we do. Although, some of us fill that hole with other, productive things such as writing (example: me, writing this lovely book for you to read), music, painting, charity work, or we seek a higher power for guidance. Regardless of the path we choose, there is no denying we have a hole where our past relationship once was. And... it must be filled.

As I stated earlier, when we run from our past, we stupidly believe that it is possible. We may begin a brand new life and successfully put on a fantastic show for our new friends to see. However, maybe tonight, tomorrow, next week, or next month, our charade will end. We will lose our resolve to ignore our past and our real, troubled selves will show their hideous faces.

Our past is who we are. If we made mistakes, those mistakes will not go away. If someone deeply hurt us, we will never forget it. Today, in our snapshot in time, we tend to believe that we can simply forget, or the mistakes we made will be forgotten, either by those we wronged or by ourselves. This will never happen and it is time we realize that.

Now that I have you depressed, let me ask the question we all want to know the answer to... what do we do now? How do we deal with the here and now, aka our snapshot? The answer is simple. We accept it. We are human. We have made mistakes. People have wronged us and hurt us. We may have hurt others. Can we take it back? No, not even a little bit. What's done is done. However, we *can* learn from it.

For most of us, this is the point where it all begins to go horribly wrong. We start to believe that something is wrong with us. We may believe no one cares for us and that we are simply unlovable. We may spiral downward into a depression if we are hurt badly enough. That, however, is not the answer. You may have just said, "Duh, this guy is an idiot." I must admit, it sounds obvious, but for those of us who have experienced such heartache, it's not obvious at all. Our pain is very real and many times it blinds us from what everyone else around us can see as plain as day. But everyone must admit our past has a huge effect on us, whether or not you want to acknowledge it.

Obviously, the vast majority of adults, or anyone with a small amount of reason, we know destructive behaviors will not solve anything. Even when we polish off that pint of cookies and cream ice cream while our salty tears taint the perfect taste of Oreos mixed in creamy ice cream, we know this is solving nothing. Yet, we do it anyway. We shove that wonderful food in our mouth and hope it will make us feel better.

I dare say that we all may need a period where we wallow in self-pity. As I consider myself a subject matter expert in self-pity, I will acknowledge that there is a time and place for such things. However, the time should most definitely be short lived and the place should be in private or surrounded by very close friends. Self-pity for the world to see does no one, especially ourselves, any good. (See Facebook statuses or Tweets.)

Actually, let me rant about Facebook statuses for one minute. I will admit that in a (usually drunken) rage, I have posted a status on Facebook about people pissing me off. At the time, I knew full well that the people I was angry with would know I was being a _____.   That kind of passive aggressive behavior is just embarrassing and stupid. I mean come on, get a grip.   There is a time and place for that nonsense and Twitter and Facebook are not those places.

Enough said. Moving on from self-pity.

At some point in our journey of wallowing in our pit of despair, we come to a fork in the road. Either we snap out of our self-destructive behavior or we continue our downward spiral. Make no mistake; this choice is usually harder than it seems on paper. Perhaps our behavior is sex. Let's be honest… sex is fun. Is meaningless sex fun? On second thought, don't answer that you horny hellions. Maybe it's ice cream… ice cream is good. Whatever it is, I challenge you that your vice of choice is simply a 'bucket.'

Imagine a small fishing boat in the middle of a lake with a hole in the bottom of the boat. You are in the boat, without any oars to row yourself to shore and to safety. Suddenly, water slowly fills up the boat and you begin to sink. You have the tools to fix the boat in front of you as well as an empty tin bucket. Most of us use the bucket out of panic. We franticly scoop up water from our sinking boat and toss it back into the lake. This slows our sinking, but does it plug the hole at the bottom of the boat? Does the water we toss out go anywhere except the same lake that is already drowning us?

Clearly, our answer is to plug that dastardly hole in our boat. While it may take longer to truly plug that hole once and for all, once it's corrected, no more water will sneak into our boat. Then, and only then, will we be able to use a bucket to free ourselves from the water that almost overtook us. Ideally, we will no longer be frantic since we are no longer sinking. Therefore, we will choose a bucket that is not a self-destructive behavior. Cause let's be honest, self-destructive behavior creates more holes more often than not. I hope that I do not have to specify the correlation to the hole in the boat to the hole left by a broken relationship, but I will anyway. Until we fix that hole for good, we are still sinking. The black water around us will continue to overwhelm us until we are underwater and about to drown. No amount of frivolous activities or denial will change that fact.

As I already mentioned in this chapter, the answer is simple (in theory) on how to fix our sinking ship. We must accept our past, our pain, and our failures. I will assume that if you are reading this, your snapshot in time is of a sinking ship. Perhaps you are up to your neck in water and taking on more? Or perhaps you have fixed your leak but are unsure where to go next? Regardless of the stage you are in, acknowledging our past is first and foremost. Without our past, who are we? It's time to accept ourselves.

Chapter 3
Running From Our Past

Let us explore why we run from our past. First, and most obviously, it's because it's easier. So much easier, it should be illegal. Why would we willingly put ourselves through our own psyche and attempt to navigate our broken hearts and warped minds? That sounds horrible! No thanks; I will just blame others instead...

Second, the reason why it's easier is because when we look at our past, we are forced to examine ourselves. None of us wants to admit defeat. None of us wants to think that we caused a relationship to fail or that we played any part in it at all. We run away so that we can look back and point the finger at someone else instead of looking at whatever role we played, no matter how small.

As we discussed in Chapter 2, our ship is sinking. If we continue to ignore the past and blame others, we will keep sinking deeper and deeper. In fact, we will create more holes in our boat or make the existing holes much bigger. Soon, we will end up so over our heads that we will do something drastic to get out. Some of us will run even farther away, hoping that fixes things (it doesn't) and some of us, hopefully, will sack up and deal with it.

Which one do you think I did after my divorce? Yes, we have arrived at that time of our relationship, as writer and reader, for me to open up and tell you a little bit about myself. Ready? Yep, I ran further away. I sure did. I made a quick decision to move away completely. Start over and hope that my past would not impact future relationships. Can you believe I was dumb enough to think no girl would ask about my past? What an idiot! I actually believed I could skate by on some nonsense answer, therefore ignoring my own past. Not my finest moment.

Point being, we can keep running away. Sure, it's easier that way for the time being. When things get more and more tough for us, we can keep running and running. This exhausts our mind, body, heart and soul. However, we will eventually have no choice but to stop running. Wait... Do you feel it? Yep, here comes another crucial turning point... When we turn around and face our past demons; when we decide to stop using our bucket and fix that pesky hole in our boat: what/who do we focus on? By now, I hope you realize the answer is not someone or something else. It's ourselves. Some of you might be thinking, "Excuse me, I was cheated on. This has nothing to do with me." Well, I hate to say it but... You. Are. Wrong. I am **not** saying anyone deserves to be cheated on. No one does. NO ONE. (Yes, I just yelled at you. See texting and social media etiquette of using all CAPS.) Even the worst boyfriend or girlfriend doesn't deserve it. No matter what they did, even if they cheated on you first. Yet, it still has everything to do with you. Let me explain.

Cheating leaves the offended feeling as if they did something wrong; that they lack something. Why else would their significant other do that? Too often, the offended believes it's their fault. That maybe you aren't good-looking enough? Aren't good enough in bed? Too fat? Too skinny? Too awesome? Again, no matter what they may or may not have done, the offended typically feels these things or something similar. However, let us be clear, **it is not your fault**. Period. Yet you are the one left feeling violated, alone, and confused as to what you did wrong. It is cruel and unfair. Unfortunately, many of us know that feeling all too well.

While we are on the topic of cheating, let's also look at the Cheater. (First of all, what a horrible word? "Cheater." The sound of it invokes a lot of hatred, doesn't it?) Having said that, I have a confession... I am a Cheater. Don't you dare judge me, because chances are, you are too. Cheating can mean many things. It can mean the obvious, which is sex with another person other than your significant other. It might mean a kiss when you got too drunk one night and don't even remember it (not an excuse by the way). It could even mean that you have cheated on someone emotionally by confiding in another when you don't do the same with your significant other. This last one is the worst by the way; far worse than something purely physical in nature. You would be hard pressed to get five people in a room together and agree on what "cheating" actually is. Try it and see what happens.

As the offended, we need to realize something about the cheating bastard in front of us. Yes, they *are* missing something from the relationship. Yes, they *may* blame us for what is missing. But know this… one day, they will realize that what is missing from the relationship is within themselves. It is not something that you should, or even could, bring to the relationship. It's the hole somewhere inside them. They have a hole in their ship that needs to be fixed. That hole has nothing to do with us, the offended. It has everything to do with them, the Cheater.

Side note. Does anyone believe in "Once a Cheater, always a Cheater?" If you said yes, you are only half-correct. A Cheater will continue the same pattern of behavior until they recognize the reasons behind their infidelity. They, like us, will blame others first. We already established this earlier…it is much easier that way. Can you honestly blame them? Do not forget we all struggle with similar, yet not identical issues. The guy who continues to cheat simply has not looked inside himself to determine what is missing inside him. The girl who loves the attention from every boy at the bar, even while her boyfriend is in awe of her, has yet to realize she is not happy with herself. 100% of the time it's the Cheater, not the offended. As the offended, we can choose to support them, but we cannot fix them. That is up to the Cheater.

A Cheater can, however, change. I have already admitted I have cheated in the past. Will I always do that? Absolutely not. Will the woman of my dreams come along and fix that? Absolutely not. It's me. It was my problem that I needed to recognize, and then address. Not my chosen partner, since it had nothing to do with them. Here we go again, I am about to share so get ready.

Even though we are all different, I will open up and tell you why I have cheated, hoping someone out there may relate. Quite simply, it's because I needed the constant validation that I was worth something. I was unhappy with myself, therefore needed outside validation of who I was. Who better to do that than a pretty girl who is fun to flirt with? It is as simple as that. I blamed my significant other for not giving me what I needed (and no, I am not talking about sex), yet I was unable to explain what it was that she wasn't giving me. I kept saying, "I don't know, you should know what I want and you aren't giving it to me." One word: Ridiculous. I wish I could say I am making this up, but I am not. I couldn't explain what she could do for me to make me happier, because she couldn't do anything for me. It was me. My problem.

It is very true; harmless flirting leads to harmful flirting. A simple kiss leads to...well...I am not going to spell it out for you, you get it. Point being, it usually starts small and even innocent and then grows into something not so innocent. Then, the "other person" becomes your bucket to save your sinking ship. However, that is all they are...a bucket. Someone else may help you feel better, or *think* you feel better, even while you may have a significant other, who is already doing the exact same thing. Our hole is like a tapeworm that can never be filled by outside sources. Doesn't matter what we try to fill it with. If it doesn't come from within ourselves, it will not work and we will keep using our bucket.

Cheating is simply one symptom of running from our pasts and our pain. That is all it is. Whether or not we want to take a second and look at cheating from the Cheaters point of view we have to admit it, the Cheater has a legitimate problem. It needs to be fixed. They need to face their past and their own shortcomings before their cheating will ever stop. However, it can stop. I truly believe that. Cheating is simply their bucket. Admittedly, it's a worse bucket than say eating an entire bag of chips while watching reruns of soap operas, but it's still a bucket. Fundamentally, that makes their sinking ship no different than yours or mine. That may be difficult to understand if you have been cheated on, but being on both sides of the argument, this is what I believe.

Back to the comment I made on how you, as the victim of cheating, are free and clear of a cheating experience. If you have been cheated on and you make the choice to walk away from that relationship, do not be fooled to think that the episode of cheating did not involve you. No, you were not the reason they cheated, but it did involve you and you were impacted in one way or another. You need to realize that and deal with it.

Although we spent a few pages on cheating, this chapter is about running from our past in general, not just cheaters. Many of us will do anything not to face our fears, especially when it will make us look weak and vulnerable. Looking inside ourselves is like pointing a gun in the mirror directly at our face. We feel like we are aiming the gun directly at ourselves and that the bullet will tear right through us and kill us. Once we pull that trigger, that mirror image of perfection that we *think* we see in front of us, will certainly shatter. A few fragments will undoubtedly come back and cut us deeply. However, when we pull that trigger, we shatter our reflection of ourselves and not our true selves. In the end, it will only make us stronger.

I know what you are thinking. "All of this is easier said than done, you jerk." You are entirely correct. I am a jerk. And it is easier said than done, too. This is probably the hardest part in this book and was, and continues to be, the hardest part of my personal journey. It takes courage to stop running. However, it has to be done. Are you ready? Well, too bad, get ready because if you can't do this, you might as well stop reading and forget the rest of this book. Here we go…

All right, slow that run of yours down to a light jog. You have been running and running and I am sure you are exhausted. Now stop jogging completely. Take a few steps while you catch your breath. Hang your head as air enters your lungs and your heart begins to slow. Now, take a deep breath. Take another one and close our eyes. You are about to face whatever it is you are running from, so take another deep breath. Lift your head up, turn around and exhale. Take one more deep breath and open those eyes.

What you see behind you, what you have been running from, is… you. Some of it you may not like, but… it is you. It is the culmination of all of our past experiences, both good and bad. Our past defines us and makes us as unique as each star in the sky. They look similar from far away, but each star has different compositions of gas and materials that orbit it. (Yes, I did just call you full of gas.) Stars take many years to form and no star forms the exact same way. Our past is unique and that is now what you are looking at. Don't turn away from it either. A quick glance doesn't count if you turn back around and keep running. It is time to face what we may have done, right or wrong, and where we have been. Doesn't matter what you did or what happened to you. We all have unique experiences to be sure, but we need to acknowledge that we are not the only one with experiences. I know it may hurt to face our past and allow the pain to return once more. However, all of it needs to be faced. And that starts now.

Chapter 4

Face the Facts, Jack

We need to keep having a frank conversation here. (As if we haven't been having one already.) So, I am going to drop some knowledge on you. Are you ready? I don't think you're ready. Now are you ready? Ok here goes...

You, my friend, are all kinds of jacked up. You have issues. You have done things that you aren't proud of. You have harmed people. You have yelled, cussed, and been way out line. Basically, you are an emotional terrorist. You are all those things and more.

Also, on the other side of the coin, you have been mistreated. Badly, I am guessing. You have cried like a baby and felt so low at times, that you had a hard time finding a reason to get out of bed in the morning. You have cried so hard that your head hurt. Your heart has been broken into millions of shattered fragments. You are all these things and more.

Now... get over it.

Next Chapter.

Kidding... kind of. WE are all those things. WE are all flawed individuals. WE are ALL jacked up. However, we truly need to get over it. If you are like me, this is not easy.

Truthfully, though, if you can't get over this, you might

as well grab some butter, cause you're toast. And not the good kind of sugar and cinnamon toast. The burnt to Hell toast that tastes like crap when you take a bite.

"Who is this guy and why did he just yell at me like that?" That is what you are thinking. It's okay. I had to do that to myself a while back. Correction, I continually have to do that to myself. As do you, I am guessing. If you haven't, then now is the time. We need to face these facts about ourselves. It's a hard pill to swallow, but we aren't perfect. And no matter how hard we try, we never will be. Not even close!

I will use the best example of these shenanigans: Myself. I am a perfectionist. When something goes wrong, I flip. If someone else messes up, I get that, mistakes happen and I let it slide. No problem, let's move on. If I mess up? Nope. Unacceptable. I expect more from myself. I expect excellence in all that I do. (Please don't insert jokes about this book and flaws you have found.) This is who I am. I hate failure. My fears in life: 1. Failure. 2. Snakes. 3. Clown cars. I even go as far to call every single dating relationship I have ever been through a failure. That is a harsh choice of word, but it's how I look at it. I ask myself, "Are you in a happy relationship right now?" My answer to me is, "No. In fact, I am not even in a crappy relationship." I say back to myself, "Exactly, hence, you failed in every relationship." I then reply, "Why am I talking to myself? I tend to do this a lot. I am going to stop now."

Point being, I am the King of self-loathing. I know what it feels like to hate yourself because a relationship didn't work out. One date or five years… doesn't matter. It was a failure to me. This means I am left feeling horrible. The vast majority of my life, I took the easy way out. "Obviously, it was them, not me." I mean, duh. I am a perfectionist, I try at everything, how could it have been me?

Let me ask you a question that I finally had to ask myself; what is the common denominator in all of your failed relationships? Think on it… is it your chosen partners? Guys, do you always date the girl who thinks she is better than everyone? Girls, do you date the douche bag, hoping you can change him? Doesn't even matter the answer to those questions, actually. Have you figured it out? Do you know what the common theme in those relationships was?

<u>YOU!</u>

Now, before you open your mouth in shock, like many of you just did, let me explain. I am not trying to offend you and get you all riled up on something. My point, again using myself as the example, is that we have past experiences and we need to get over them and learn from them. If we can't learn from them and move on, then every relationship moving forward is doomed. We agreed you can't run from your past, so it's time to turn around and face it.

First up… ourselves. This one is the tough one. Like me, many of you think, "I didn't do anything wrong, dude. Move on to the next topic." It's true, you may not have made some grave error that caused your relationship to stumble and fall. You may be the victim of a cheater, for example. You may have been treated badly and decided to leave a toxic relationship. In any case, walking away is much easier said than done and we owe it to ourselves to make sure we are okay, even when we think we are.

As I said before, I carry each defeat with me as a failure. Perhaps I am unique in that way. Maybe I am not. Or maybe you carry it with you and you don't realize it? Each time we enter a relationship, we open ourselves up to another person. Most of us start small and let it grow. But even a small opening can let feelings in and out. Do not make the mistake of thinking that you walked away from a failed relationship without any damage done to your soul. You are an idiot if you think that.

We must, MUST, forgive ourselves. This can be easier (not easy) if you truly were the "victim" in the failed relationship. Yet, we still need to say to ourselves, "I did my best, and it didn't work. I will learn from this and apply it to my next relationship." Or you might be a person who would say this; "I didn't try at all. I didn't even care what happened. Now I know why it failed." Either way, we need to be honest with ourselves and recognize our part of responsibility for the relationship not working, no matter how small it may be.

Some people have no trouble with this at all. But make no mistake, whether consciously or unconsciously; they reconcile their shortcomings in the relationship that just failed. They are lucky, lucky people to be able to do that so quickly. I am certainly not one of them and most likely, if you are one of those people; you are laughing your ass off reading this book.

Now, in most relationships there is the Initiator and the Reactor. Many times the Initiator did something wrong (cheating, lying, general debaucherous behaviors) and the Reactor simply...reacts. Profound, I know. Both persons must deal with what happened and move on. Both are equally difficult depending on your personality. And if you haven't figured this out yet, most, if not all, of us have been both the Initiator and Reactor. Luckily, this book is for both kinds of people since at any given snapshot we can be both.

We have already discussed the example of cheating and how the Reactor is not responsible for the Initiators actions. The Reactor must make an effort to realize this, and therefore absolve themselves of any responsibility of the Initiators actions. It sounds silly to those of you who have not been cheated on, but in this scenario, the Reactor (the one who was cheated on) still needs to forgive themselves.

We carry that weight with us. We do. Don't try to fight that fact.

The Initiator... no matter what you did, how horrible it made you feel and how much people hated you after it, you need to forgive yourself. You made a mistake. You absolutely did. Nothing can be done about that past mistake. Realize this, because without this realization you will never be happy. I make no guarantees out of this book besides this next statement. You will never be happy until you forgive yourself. Your past mistakes are mistakes that are in the past.

Another side note - forgiveness is often blurred with excusing past behavior. Um, no. Those are two mutually exclusive things. Excusing past behavior means whatever the person did was okay, and therefore can do it repeatedly. No consequences at all for their actions. Forgiveness is saying, "something bad occurred, and while I don't agree with what happened and I am hurt by it, I accept that it happened and I am willing to let it go."

That may sound like I am saying someone should stay with a cheater/liar/etc. even after they have cheated/lied/etc. I am not saying that at all. As the Reactor, you have the choice on how to behave after the Initiator starts the problem. My point is that both parties must forgive themselves at the very least. I am not going to tell you that you have to forgive the other party. But I will point out that once you forgive yourself and truly come to peace with whatever may have occurred in your relationship, the more likely you are to forgive the other person for their shortcomings; usually without even knowing it. It just happens naturally.

I am going to make a bold statement: All of the problems we keep a tight hold on lie within us. Let me elaborate. Life is not about what happens to us. It is about how we react to life. Yes, we may have been mistreated. But get over it. I have been mistreated. Everyone has been mistreated. Yes, all of us have unique stories and varying degrees of pain we have dealt with. Yet, we all have some pain, some past, and some forgiveness to ask of ourselves. Without it, we are doomed to repeat past failures and even create new problems.

I am tired of using myself as an example so I will use my friend, John. John cheated and lied to his fiancé. For six months, this happened. (How can someone do that? Be careful not to judge, we do not know John's past and what he has been through.) Yet, he came clean. He asked for forgiveness and his fiancé responded, "In time, I can forgive you." He loved his fiancé so this was acceptable to him. The wedding went on, the problems were swept under the rug hoping that time would heal all wounds. On the honeymoon, they had a horrible time, which set the stage for the rest of their marriage. For a year, he did everything he could to prove to his new bride that he wanted to be with her. Things he denied her in the past (email records, phone records, passwords to social media) he gave her. Anything she wanted.

After a year of this, he finally agreed to go to marriage counseling. Marriage counseling led to one-on-one counseling for John. He said he learned a lot about his patterns of behavior and applied what he learned the best he knew how. His wife even accompanied him to counseling a few times.

However, after a year and half, his wife moved out of their house. Everything he was doing to wipe away his past sins, was not working. Those were his wife's words, not his. His wife said that she needed time away from him and signed a lease somewhere else. John was heartbroken and did not understand what else he could do. Obviously, we all see what he did... he cheated on his fiancé, which anyone can agree was horrible. Ultimately, he had enough rejection from the one who promised to love him forever for better or worse. Together, they decided divorce was the only option and within three months of his wife moving out, their marriage was over.

Was John in the wrong? Absolutely. Was his wife in the wrong? Absolutely. From John's point of view, two years later he is still dealing with the pain he dealt with before they pledged to love each other for better or for worse. Still, he knows he messed up before they were married. He also knows he made the right decisions to fix what he did by going to counseling. Yet, it wasn't enough. For a man, that is a tough burden to bear. He still carries that with him to this day.

Finally, he was able to do the unthinkable and forgive himself. Again, not excuse himself from what he did, but forgive himself. He made a mistake. A big one. But he decided to turn things around and start doing the right thing. Most of what he was doing in his marriage wasn't working because he hadn't forgiven himself. Now that he has, he can look to the future and to what he can change the next time he is ready to try another meaningful relationship.

His wife? She made the mistake of thinking time would heal those wounds he caused. Time may heal all wounds, but you are still left with a scar. A gnarly scar in this particular case. You will unfortunately carry a scar with you forever, if the wound was deep enough. We must be able to look at our scars, whether they were self inflicted (John) or done to us (John's wife) and realize that we must accept what happened. She never accepted what happened, and therefore was unable or unwilling to notice all the positive changes John had made.

That is where John's wife was in the wrong. He confided in me that she swore they would be happy before they were married. He had every reason to believe her.

Why not? She said all she needed was time and walked down the aisle to marry him. Yet, she didn't take her vows as serious as John. John's behaviors before they were married were inexcusable, but John's wife behaviors during their marriage are just as inexcusable.

No matter what it is in our past we are running from, we must face it. Realize that what happened, happened. It can't be changed. Only the here and now can be changed. Forgive yourself for whatever it was that you could have done better or for whatever it was that someone did to you. At the end of the day, placing blame on others only defers the inevitable truth that we must deal with our pain and move on.

I challenge you and myself to simply: Accept it. The reason it is our fault for prolonging our problems and pain is because we are choosing not to accept it. We can't change what we did (the case of John) or what happened to us (the case of John's wife), but we can decide what to do with that pain. We can face the facts, learn from our mistakes and pain (John), or we can choose to ignore it and never allow forgiveness (John's wife) and be miserable in a relationship.

I implore you to examine yourself and forgive. Not excuse, but forgive. It's time to let it go.

Chapter 5
The Scars of Pain

Now that we have decided to accept our pain and our past... what do we do with it? What is next? First, we need to realize that we all feel pain differently and therefore deal with it differently. As I said in the introduction, I did not study anything writing this book. I am simply pouring my heart out and sharing my thoughts. Therefore, I am not going to be a phony and make up some fancy-smancy way to describe this. I want to keep it simple for us.

A few questions to consider: Do you shut down when times get tough? Do you just stop talking and sulk? Do you get angry and yell at others? Do you not know when to walk away and let an issue lie for a minute? Do you try to find the answers for your pain at the bottom of a bottle? Maybe inside a greasy hamburger wrapper? How do you deal with your pain? And how do you react to the way others around you deal with their pain?

Even more important than how 'do you deal with the pain,' is which way actually works? And I don't mean temporarily. Again, I feel as if this is my confession, but I admit that I have temporarily sought solace out of the bottom of a bottle. No, I was never and I am not currently an alcoholic. I did, however, choose to drink rather than face my problems many days. Did it work? Truthfully, yes, it did;

but not for long. Soon, the buzz wore off and not only was my pain still there; I now had a hangover as a consolation prize. That wasn't the answer that worked for me. It was merely a Band-Aid over a gushing wound. Or more precisely, it was my bucket to my sinking ship.

In case you are wondering what worked for me... you are reading it. Writing works for me. If I were having a particularly bad day with confronting my past, I would write about it. Or I would write about how I felt when I looked back at my past, what I did, or what I had been through. Writing helped me find the exact feelings I was dealing with, or more specifically, trying to ignore. I will share a few poems throughout the rest of this book as examples.

Writing may not work for everyone. In fact, it probably won't. This part of the journey is where we tend to give up and revert back to using our buckets. Although we already made the hard decision to turn and face our past, now we must actually stick with it. This is not easy either. It is much easier to turn back around when the pain comes rushing over us like a tsunami. But then you are back where you started, and many times you are actually worse off.

So what do we do? Sadly, trial and error is the only way I know how. If you are a creative person, go to a craft store and buy a large canvas and paint. Then splatter the snot out of that canvas with all of your pain inside. Let loose! If you have a lot of pent up anger, take up running or boxing.

Do something physical. They key here is to channel your anger/frustration/pain into something worthwhile. Drinking, drugs, and other unscrupulous behavior might provide some relief for a minute. However, be prepared to have it all come rushing back at you since those self-destructive behaviors are only temporary and leave you worse off than when you started.

While you perform your chosen method of coping, think back on who has hurt you. Think back on what they did that broke your heart and how that made you feel. This is tough, but it needs to be done. Realize that whatever they did, they did because it was their choice to do so. It does not reflect on you as a person or on your ability to be a good significant other. It was them, and their choice had nothing to do with you, therefore you had, and never will, have control over it.

Box up all of those hurt feelings and that deep pain into one huge box. Now, let it go. Actually, don't let it go. Dropkick it! Why hold on to it? What are you getting from it? More pain… that is what. You cannot change how people acted towards you or what they did to you. So let it go. I will say it again; it was them, not you.

If you were actually able to do that, well done. I bet you can take a deep breath and you feel like something has been lifted off your shoulders and your heart. If you were unable to do this… you better go back to page one and start again cause you missed something. You are sent back to your room without dinner, so start all over from the beginning. We will see you back here when you are done.

Is everyone ready to move on?

Although that was tough, this next part is worse. Time to deal with the pain we have caused internally. This could mean a few different things. It could mean dealing with the pain that we know we hurt someone we deeply care about. In the case of John, most of his pain was dealing with knowing how much he hurt his fiancé/wife. For others, it could be self-internalized pain we created. Maybe you blame yourself and only yourself for the failure of your relationship. That's a heavy burden to bear, especially since that way of thinking is all kinds of wrong. It takes two to make a relationship work and I believe that it takes two to make it fall apart. It is not always 50/50, but it still takes two.

If you have created blame for yourself to rationalize the fact that maybe someone decided to stop being with you… you're an idiot. Mostly kidding, but truthfully, it's not you. It was them. (I am going to keep repeating myself until we all get it) We will discuss this in more detail later, but the key to remember is that not everyone is compatible. That is okay. You don't have to be perfect for everyone, which is good since you can't be. But - more on this later.

Do not take the entire blame on yourself. Ever! Remember that we recognized we are human and we make mistakes. We made a mistake. Maybe a few of them. That doesn't condemn us, we are allowed to mess up from time to time. (Yes, as a perfectionist, this is hard to admit and I am saying this to myself just as much as I am saying it to you.) I know it is easier said than done, but the only way to forgive ourselves is to acknowledge all of the pain we have been carrying around. Acknowledge it, and then let it go.

A great example of this is back to my friend John. He made a mistake; he apologized for it and finally forgave himself. He also must realize that his wife made the mistake of choosing to declare her love and devotion to him for all eternity, all the while knowing she didn't mean those words. She made that choice to not forgive John and to move out. Sure, John messed up, but the fault is not entirely his.

Here is the first of my poems I want to share. I wrote this as I was trying to come to terms with the pain I continued to feel, even though I didn't understand where it was coming from:

Someone please take away all this pain
Each morning brings a new layer of stain
It takes all I have to breathe and stay afloat
Seems like no one else is in the same boat

The world doesn't seem to care at all
They all just watch as I stumble and fall
It gets harder and harder to stand back up
The longer I tread, the deeper I'm stuck

I think I find someone to guide me through the dark

But all I find is lies from the very start
There must be something wrong with me
What is it that I am choosing not to see

Where am I supposed to go from here
All that surrounds me is anxiety and fear
These walls keep closing closer in
These days it feels like I will never win

What did I do to deserve this
All I can ever do is swing and miss
I highly doubt I can take much more
I feel like there is more of this in store

I just arrived but all I want is to run
Head straight and deep inside the sun
All of this seems a waste in vain
All I am is stuck with all this pain

Take a guess at when I wrote that uplifting piece. Your guess might be while I was going through my divorce or immediately after. Nope. It was months after, while I was "having the time of my life" partying like it was going out of style. Deep down, I had a lot pain. I was choosing to mask it. Not allowing myself to deal with it in any shape or form. I read that poem now and I can vividly remember how I felt the day I wrote it. Those painful scars will always be there to remind me what I have been through. It has made me who I am today, just as what you have been through has made you who you are today.

Stop running from it. Accept the wrongs that people have done to you and the wrongs you have inflicted on others. Take that pain and literally let it run all over you like a stampeding bull. It's going to hurt, but it needs to be done if you haven't done it already.

Go ahead, I will wait...

How did that feel? Horrendous? Like bamboo shoved under your fingernails? Good, then it worked. Recognize that pain and make the decision right now to let it go. It is a toxic substance within your soul and it will eat you alive from the inside. It will not, simply will not go away on its own. Now is the time to put that bucket aside and fix that hole inside us. The pain we have held on to has muddied the water inside our sinking boat. We were unable to see where the hole was to fix it. Now, we can see that hole and fix ourselves.

Admit to yourself that we all make mistakes and it's time to move on. It's time to forgive, but not forget. Don't resent yourself or your past for who it made you today. It has created you. Cherish the fact that you have the power and ability to face your past, while not allowing that same past and pain to control you. From now on, this is who you are. This is who we are.

My hope is that you are able to do that and let the pain go. No longer will it control you and who you are. It certainly has helped sculpt who you are today, but it will not control what you do from now on. Yes, we are left with scars that we will carry forever, but as time goes on those scars will fade.

The toxic essence of pain is gone, which allows us a great ability to grow and learn from our past. The rest of this book will focus on just that; our future. Now that we have freed ourselves from our pain, it is time to start looking forward.

Chapter 6
Situational Love and Hate

I have a theory. Actually, I have many theories on many different topics, but since this book is about love and relationships, I will stick to the lesson plan. My theory on love is that when two people come together and decide to start a relationship, there is one factor that is more important than anything else. It's not religion, politics, ethics or anything of that nature. People's opinions of those things tend to change over time anyway. What determines if a couple will be successful is simply: timing.

The purpose of this chapter is to prepare us for what we are about to encounter in the dating world and maybe shed some light on why other relationships may not have worked. For me, and maybe those of you reading this book, we are repairing ourselves and rebuilding our hearts for a better and brighter future. However, before we can do that, we need to understand the concept of timing.

Let me ask you this; have you ever broken up with someone (or been broken up with) because you and your significant other were "at different places?" It sounds like a copout, doesn't it? I don't believe that it is. I believe it is everything. A perfect example is a girl I knew throughout high school and college. I was this girl's first kiss and we "dated" (whatever you want to call seeing each other when you can't legally drive) for a few weeks, but it wasn't really anything special since we were so young. However, we hung out in the same circles so we continued to run into one another. Every time I was single, I would give her a call. She always had a boyfriend. When she was single, she called me and I had a girlfriend. This went on for ten years! Even to this day, I talk to her every now and again. We both recognize that we liked each other and something was there, but our timing was off. Way off.

The previous example shows how I was not even able to attempt a relationship with someone that I was interested in because of timing. However, what if you are already dating someone and after a few dates, you find that you are in different places in life? I will be honest and say that I have used that exact reasoning to stop seeing someone. Was it a copout? I stand firm in saying it absolutely was not.

Within the past year, in fact, I really liked someone but at the point I was at in life, I was very different from the girl I was dating. For me, it was that I was coming out of a serious relationship (a marriage) and for her, she wanted in one (again, a marriage). Would she have been a fantastic girlfriend? There is no doubt in my mind that she would have been and that I would be happy with her. Yet, I was smart enough (for once) to recognize that no matter how much we liked each other, we caught each other at different points in our lives. Sometimes there isn't anything you can do about that.

But what does that even mean? Does it make me a bad person because I don't want a girlfriend? Does it make her clingy since she wants a boyfriend? Not at all. It just means we want different things. I will want a girlfriend in the future and if I run into her at that point, then you bet your bottom dollar I will ask her out again. My situation might have changed by then. To be fair, I run the risk that her situation may have changed as well. Point being, you need to take stock of what we are willing to risk given the fact that the two of you might not be at the same place in your "relationship life."

The best possible example for timing is the classic "rebound." Who among us has not had, or tried to find, a rebound? We were hurt, so we looked for someone to fill our void (can you say, "bucket" anyone?) A rebound is exactly what I am talking about here. All it is is timing. When you met that rebound, you (probably) lowered your standards just because you are at a time where you need a new companion. Most of us looking in from the outside can see it, and you can't. I have a friend who is probably the best-looking girl I have ever met. Literally. No exaggeration. She had a boyfriend when I met her, then they broke up a few months later. I will be honest; I tried to insert myself more into her life so I could get a feel for what she was looking for.

I quickly found out that she was already dating someone else. Then, I saw the guy. My reaction was, "Are you freaking kidding me right now?" The guy was a tool.

What could I do? Nothing. She didn't see what she was doing so I told myself this: "The fact that I wanted to date this girl and she ended up dating a bozo, is not because this dude is better than me, it is because he fit her needs at the exact time that she needed it. I am not inferior to that guy, it was simply a matter of timing."

Here is another example from my chronicles of love (or lack-there-of). A few weeks ago, my buddy and I were at a crowded bar just having a grand ole time. We like to be sociable and talk to people. When I say people, I mean beautiful women. Anyway, we see two women walk by and give us the 'eye' (or so we thought). We were standing up surveying the room and they go sit down at the only table still open. What would any two, single guys do? Obviously, we immediately walk over to them and sit down at their table with them.

I walk over and say, "Hi, how are you ladies this evening?" By the way, it's not the best pick up line, but it's better than something dumb that makes me look like I rehearsed it. So don't judge.

One of the girls responded, without any sense of hesitation, "We just want to be left alone tonight."

My response, "....."

I look at the other girl at the table. Her face tells me that what her friend said was true, but it might not be a decision they agreed upon together. I look at my buddy, who looks just as flabbergasted as I was at what was occurring here. I had never been told that!

Seeing as how it was later in the night (after a few drinks), I did not react appropriately. After I picked my jaw up from the floor, I responded, "Congratulations for bitch of the night award. You two ladies have fun, being at a crowded bar on a Saturday night, not talking to anyone." Then we walked off. Again, I probably shouldn't have said that… but it was funny at the time. Still is, actually. But, I digress.

In case you were wondering what she said, she said nothing. I am fairly confident she knew she was rude. They left the bar about 5 minutes after our pleasant interaction.

Nevertheless, that package of joy I tried to talk to did not react to me the way she did because of who I am. It wasn't that I had an over-the-top pickup line or I was wearing overalls at a fancy bar. It was because whatever situation she was in that night, was not the situation I was in. I was looking for fun and conversation. She wasn't. That truthfully doesn't make her a bad person or a bitch (as I called her). And it doesn't make me a bad person for approaching her, either. What I said back to her… well… that is a different story. But still, my story shows that mine and this girls interaction was not because of who we are, it was because of 'where' we are. If you are following me, you understand I don't mean that particular bar we were in that night. I am referring to our state of minds.

So what determines the "place" we are in at any given time? Is it our maturity level? Mood? Financial situation? Family dynamics? The placement of the moon? The answer is, yes; all of it. Except maybe the moon, unless you read and believe your horoscope each day. Or, unless you are a werewolf, in which case you have a whole lot of other problems to figure out. Everything we have been through, the pain we have endured, and finally, freed ourselves from, has brought us here.   Our situation is unique; just as everyone else has a unique situation.

The loathing I received from the girl at the crowded bar, was situational hate. It wasn't me she hated; it was whatever situation she was in. And I had no idea what that situation was and I should have given her a break. Honestly, I should have said this, "You know what? I see that you must be going through some things in your life. I respect that and understand that you may not be in the mood for idle chatter. I hope you and your friend have a great night and if you change your mind and want to talk, we will be right over there."

How classic would that have been? I guarantee we would have walked away and she would have looked at her friend to hear her say, "You just turned away the only genuine guys in this bar." That isn't my point, though that totally would have worked. Point being, just as no one truly understands our exact circumstances, we are unable to understand theirs either.

On the flip side of this example, I have another cautionary tale. Just as we can be a victim, or perpetrator, of situational hate, we can be the same in situational love. Situational love isn't even real love, but often times we believe it is. And again, I am a wonderful example of what not to do.

I had just come out of my marriage. I was distraught, lonely, and breaking apart. I found safety in an old flame, which I began talking to more and more. It was nice to talk to her and reconnect on a personal level. If that were the end of the story, then life would have been good. But, no, of course it doesn't end there. This is me we are talking about. Do you see the pattern I finally saw? Anyway, moving on...

I began thinking that since this girl was giving me some attention after my marriage, she was the answer to all my problems. Harmless flirting turned into nightly calls and text messages about how much I liked her. She reciprocated from time to time, but not nearly on the same level as I was.

I continued to "fall for her" and would do anything to see her, including very long car rides to the city she lived in.

Yep, we didn't even live in the same city. I was grasping for something that wasn't even there.

Finally, she began to tell me over and over again, "I can't be what you need right now."

My response was, "Nonsense, you are exactly what I need right now."

I hate to admit it, but her rejecting me was the best thing that could have happened to me at that point. I wasn't in love with her. I didn't want to start a long distance relationship with someone. However, the situation I was in at that exact moment made me vulnerable. I grabbed on to something I thought I needed. At the time, it truly broke my already torn apart heart. Yet, it was the right decision on her part to turn me away.

Who really broke my heart though? Was it her? I don't think so. It was actually me. She saw the bigger picture and knew that she was the "rebound" and that I was acting this way merely because of the situation I was in. Had she just got out of a relationship, perhaps she would have been in the same place. Yet again, timing is everything and thankfully, for both her and I, we were in different places.

My view, is that just like situational hate isn't "fair" (queue the girl saying, "no thanks, we don't want to be talked to tonight"), neither is situational love. I would argue that rebound relationships don't usually last long. I could be totally wrong here, and maybe someone found their spouse in a rebound relationship... but I am still sticking to my guns. I doubt situational love works often, because our situation dictates what love means to us. Usually, we are jaded (hate) or vulnerable (looking for any kind of love), which creates these situations we find ourselves in.

Overall, we need to realize that there are times when we, and others, might be in a specific situation and we, and others, should give each other a break. As we enter this dating world, be prepared to understand this fact. I suggest that we act not like me and the girl at the bar, and not like me and the old flame I tried to turn into my own personal savior and do our best to recognize these situations before they get out of control.

Instead of falling victim to situational love or hate, we need to practice situational awareness. Know your weaknesses that you are working on right now and don't fall prey to them. I don't mean your weakness for tall, dark and handsome or for the blonde with large breasts. Don't allow others who aren't as enlighten as we are, to derail your journey forward. Simply be aware of who we are, where you are, and where you want to go. Know that others may or may not be at the place you are right now. And that is perfectly okay. That makes us different, it doesn't make one better than the other.

Now that we are aware of our current situation, let's take stock of what we are now able to accomplish. Not just accomplish, but also successfully achieve.

Chapter 7

Put Me In Coach

Up to this point, we have been the backup quarterback in our own football game. We fumbled, we goofed up, read the wrong coverage or we got sacked so hard we needed to be taken out of the game. We have been sitting on the edge of the bench, helmet off, mud on our face while rain pours down all over us. Finally, we caught our breath. It's time to raise our head and put that helmet back on.

But how? For some, brushing yourself off is enough. For others, we need to sit on the bench and watch others take our starting roles. We need the humility of sitting out for a few plays, perhaps longer.

While we have been sitting on the bench, we have recognized what we have been through, reminisced on past relationships, faced our own demons, as well as what others may have done to us. We have dealt with our pain and made the decision to get rid of it and fix what may have caused the pain to begin with (forgiving others) or what caused us to hold on to that pain (ourselves).

I hate to break it to you; it is not as easy as running back on the field and trying again. It takes courage. Not a little bit, a lotta bit. To be clear, some of us need time on the bench. Some of us need to sit out of the game for a minute longer than someone else. And that's okay. It doesn't make us weak. It makes us cautious. There is nothing wrong with taking time to be sure you are ready to go back into the game we call "dating."

Although we have made a lot of progress, we are not done. We forgave ourselves, but are we happy? Do you "need" someone to make you feel happy or special? Do you "have" to be back in the dating pool to be happy? If the answer is yes to either one of those questions, my assertion is that you are not ready to come off the bench just yet.

We owe it to ourselves, and to others, to be complete. The phrase, "you complete me" is total horse manure. Sorry, but it's true. Neither I, nor anyone should ever need someone else to be complete. If that were the case, I would constantly need someone around to make me feel special. As we discussed earlier, where does that lead? Cheating, for one.

We need to find ourselves before we can go back in the game. We need to know who we are, and more importantly, we need to be comfortable with that. No, forget that, we need to be proud of it. We are a culmination of our past and we shouldn't shy away from that. Certain portions of our past may be a blemish on an otherwise pristine record, but we have already forgiven ourselves. And how can we expect others to forgive us if we haven't forgiven ourselves?

So, who are you? What are the defining moments in your life, not just in terms of relationships, that have formed you into the man or woman you are today? I'll go first... (would you expect anything less?)

I am a 30-year-old, divorced man. I have one dog, which I love more than anything and tell her that she is the only woman I believe in at the moment. I struggle with being open and honest with women, because I am afraid of their reactions. I form a wall to protect myself at any hint of trouble in the air. I often shut down entirely, rather than work on a problem within a relationship because I don't trust that people are trustworthy and will use my weaknesses against me. However, I now recognize these facts, and I am willing to do my best to work on them.

Wow. That just happened.

What about you? Do you know what being in a relationship with you would look like? How would the other person feel? Are you happy with that answer? Do you recognize your shortcomings? Trust me, it is better to realize them now, admit them to yourself, and begin working on them before they drop a bomb and leave a path of destruction on any future relationships.

I repeat, it is acceptable that we have issues. It's okay that we aren't perfect. We never will be. The question is, are we aware of our imperfections? Are we aware of what we can do to work on them? My stance is that as long as you are conscious of those things, you are on the right track. Doesn't matter where you have been or what you did in the past. We got rid of all that remember? The here and now is what matters.

That being said, it is time to be content with ourselves. We have already done the hard work in the previous pages. Be happy. No, seriously... be happy! You accomplished something. You overcame the fear of yourself. Be content with what you have and who you are. If you aren't happy and content, I can guarantee that your next relationship will fail. Take that to the bank, my friend. We must be happy with ourselves, before we can truly be happy with someone else.

It also isn't fair to whatever poor soul you end up dating. They become your self-esteem. When they aren't around, or perhaps have a bad day, you lose steam, develop a wandering eye, or begin to think you don't want to date them anymore. They don't deserve that and neither do you. You will end up back on page one again. Literally, I will make you read this book again.

By now, you know me... I write. Sometimes well and other times... don't comment on that. Anyway, after I became comfortable with my divorce and the aftermath it left, I made the decision to date again. I was nervous, didn't know if I was ready. So, while I figured it out, I wrote. I wrote exactly what I was feeling. Part of me didn't even know what I was feeling until I wrote it down. When I started writing, I wasn't sure I wanted to date yet. By the time I was finished, I had made up my mind. Within an hour, I had my first real date scheduled for a few days later (more on this later). Enjoy:

I've been standing on a cliff, toes hanging over the side as my knees tremble with fear
Over the edge, lies familiar yet terrifying territory that has eluded me every time before
Paralyzed by fear, I am afraid my leap will once again fall short of victory
Crumbling under my torn and battered feet, my mountain of protection falls apart piece by piece
My palms begin to sweat as my narrowed gaze widens with each breath
Will I conquer this hurdle and make it to the other side unscathed?
Or will I stumble and fall once again, leaving more of me unwilling to trust, to believe, or to love?
Who will catch me on the other side if I continue to miss my mark?
The weight of my self-doubt bears down on my shoulders, matched only by the pain in my soul
The road behind me is blocked, the gap must be crossed, yet is today the day?
Tonight, can I inhale all my hopes and dreams, reach the other side and exhale my past demons?
Or will my past transgressions continue to haunt and control my future?
Without a web of protection, I must forgive myself and allow me to once again be me
I understand the shackles that restrain me are of my own accord
I alone, have the rusted key of freedom hidden deep below my façade of composure
One last turn of the head as I acknowledge where I came from, appreciating the lessons learned

Looking ahead, I believe I will reach the other side, healed and awaiting new opportunities
Peering down the abyss below, I recognize though I may stumble, I will never fall that deeply again
My tears wash away my fear as grace saves me from myself once again
Feeling the cool air on my unrestrained skin, I begin to feel alive and to be believe I have it within me
Petrified of another failure I close my eyes and allow the fear inside one last time
With opened and renewed fervor, I ready myself for the long journey ahead
Unknown outcomes await me at every turn, yet no longer afraid I welcome the challenge
Surefooted, I will reach the other side and overcome my own insecurities as they attempt to defy me

Can you do that? Can you unlock the shackles of yourself and jump to the other side? Are you ready? Are you ready to take one last deep breath, put that helmet back on and run to the sidelines, waiting for your chance to get in the game? If not, that's perfectly okay. Stay seated. You are better off on the bench and that does not at all mean you aren't as good as those who are on the field. One day, your time will come. Don't rush it.

If you are ready, then what are you waiting for? Get up and await the opportunities that are already waiting for you. Tell your coach, which by the way is your heart and soul, that you're ready. You can do this. We can do this. It won't be easy, and you might get tackled back to the ground again. That's ok. If you do, you can learn another way to avoid that 300-pound defensive tackle the next time. We haven't come this far for nothing. Let's go.

Chapter 8
Playing the Game

Writing the first line of the first paragraph of this chapter, I am pretty excited. I have a feeling this might be the best chapter in this book. If not the best, at least it will be fun. This is when we get our mojo back. We get to be strong again. And we get to have fun! Let's get going, shall we?

We're back in the game now, aren't we? Feels good. We accomplished a lot so far and I am happy and content. How about you? (Better answer yes, or I will refer you to the previous chapter and back to the bench) We need to setup a few ground rules before we start:

First, I am not going to give you any magical advice to find your perfect mate. If you remember, I have yet to find that myself, so I don't have the magic answer. And by the way, there is no magic answer. So get that idea out of your head right now.

Second, this should be fun. If you aren't having fun in the dating world, you're doing something wrong. Basically, you got yourself another problem if that's the case. I am not saying it will be all roses, but overall, this is the time to get out and meet people. Enjoy yourself. Enjoy others. You deserve it. We deserve it.

Third, I am going to keep referring to dating as a 'game.' Truthfully, I don't believe in playing games with people. I can certainly do it, but I learned that when we play games, we not only hurt ourselves, but we are hurting people around us. Therefore, take the word 'game' lightly, all right folks? Don't play with people's emotions.

What other rules do we need to establish? Obviously, the most important one is to be honest with yourself, as well as with others. I do not, however, suggest that you go up to someone and act like you are performing a confession to a priest. You can if you want to, but please tell your friends before you do that. My guess is that they will want to watch that go down.

However, there is a big difference between hiding something, and deciding when to share it. I certainly don't go up to women and lead off with, "Hi, I am Clint. I'm divorced and have a difficult time trusting women. By the way, what lovely eyes you have." When the time is right, however, I bring it up. There have been a few women I dated for a few weeks and didn't even tell them I have been married. It just didn't feel right to share. No, I did not purposefully not tell them, I just didn't find the right time. And I think I made the right decision since if you were paying attention, it only lasted a few weeks anyway. Anyway, I digress, while I am not proud of my divorce, I am no longer ashamed of it either. It's a part of me and I will certainly share it with people when the time is right.

What exactly do I mean by, "when the time is right?" Well, that time is relative. It will be different for every circumstance and every potential partner. As I said before, I dated a girl for weeks without telling her I was divorced. But some girls I meet, I tell them right off the bat before I even get to the, "Can I have your number" part of the evening. Point being, there is no set of rules you must follow. You simply need to listen to yourself and allow your newly renewed heart to tell you when the time is right to share.

Now what? Let's say you share something and you're nervous what the response will be. Sound familiar? If not, you are basically lying to yourself. Here is the best part... who cares?! If the other person decides to react by walking away or being rude... fine! You don't want them anyway! That is a reflection on them and where they are in their emotional journey. Not you. You have come to terms with who you are. The fact that they may decide to walk away and be closed minded, well that is their problem. Let them walk away. Don't yell a hateful comment to them, you will only validate what they "think" of you anyway. And chances are, you were at the same place in time they were in the not so recent past as well. Allow them to walk away while you smile, knowing you are leaps and bounds ahead of them in this game we call dating.

Don't hide something that will come out eventually. Don't lie. Don't misrepresent yourself as something you're not. Someone will like you for who you are. And if they don't, isn't that their loss? As we discussed before, not everyone is compatible and that doesn't mean two incompatible people are bad people. It simply means those people shouldn't be in a relationship together.

How do you tell, though? How do you tell if you are compatible with something? That's where it gets fun. Go out! Talk to people. Grab a friend or two to join in the fun. Or better yet, don't. They may want to talk to the person who was looking at you from across the bar. That would mess up your game. Step out of your comfort zone!

During the introduction, I spoke briefly about the new world of communication we now reside in. Facebook, Twitter; instant gratification everywhere we look. Basically, these things have ruined us. Ruined us, I tell you! If it takes work, this is when we tend to say, "No thanks, I will go for something easier." Most of the time, we aren't fulfilled with that easier option either. It was too easy!

Let's talk about me since I do it so well. I consider myself pretty smooth on first dates. In fact, if I can get a girl to go on a first date with me, 9 times out of 10 I will get a second date. I am not being boastful. I never said I could get a 3rd date, 4th, 5th, or so on. The reason? First dates last a few hours, usually, right? I can be charming, funny, and sweet for a few hours. I can even ignore those ten text messages and Facebook messages I got during that time too. But eventually, the conversation turns from your favorite TV shows and how cute you look tonight, to what your family life is like or whether or not you believe in God and so forth. In other words, it gets real. That is when my generation starts to think, "Wait a minute. If everything isn't perfect from the start, I would rather just start over."

Why not? We can go on Facebook or Match.com and do a little cyberstalking. It's much easier to "wink" at someone through Match.com than to go talk to someone face to face. So, that is what many of us do. And if they don't respond within a few hours, or even worse, a day, then forget it! We are programmed to think that if we aren't perfectly happy immediately, then we never will be. This is where previous generations look at us and shake their head in disappointment. And they have every right too.

As said in the introduction, we could spend time look at the reasons "why" but ultimately, there is no point to that. We will still end up back here with the same problem. And that problem is that we are horrible at communication. Horrible.

Example: How long till you call (in reality, we don't call, we text) someone after you get their phone number? A few hours? Days? Weeks? Never? First - if we got their phone number. Don't be an idiot. Text them. If someone asks for your number and you don't have any interest in hearing from them. Say so! Don't be rude about it, just say,

"I don't think that is a good idea for me at this time." However, there is no need to be a &@!^% and roll your eyes at their poor attempt.

And by the way ladies, do you have any idea how difficult it is for a guy to ask you for your phone number? It's incredibly hard (that's what she said). Seriously, give a guy some credit just for asking.

If you do have an interest, then show it for heaven's sake. We all play the "How long till I reply back" game, don't we? That's dumb. To be clear, there are general rules to that, but I am not interested in sharing those if you don't know already. My point is that we shouldn't play by these dumb rules. If you want to talk to someone, talk to them. Why wait? Why play that game?

Let's say you go out on a date. Or even less than that, let's say you are talking to someone for an hour at bar or something. If it reaches the point where you realize you have no interest in continuing the conversation, then end it. Don't be a jackass and walk away mid-sentence, but politely say, "You know, I think you are a lovely person but I don't think this is what I am looking for." I bet the other person will be surprised, but would you rather do that or drag out your, and their, evening in a conversation that isn't going to go anywhere? Worse case, lie and say you're going to the restroom and book it. However, I suggest honesty from the start.

On the flip side, if you end up liking someone then let me just say, "slow it down cowboy." Some of us have a tendency to just jump in with both feet in without even looking. We dip our toe in the water and decide this is the best place to take a plunge. Maybe it is, but take it slow and be mindful of your current situation. Also be mindful that you are only half of the equation here. Don't make the mistake of thinking that the person you like at the moment has the exact same snapshot as you do. That is very rare. A true, well-rounded relationship can flourish when each partner learns to grow together. If one person is dragging the other along, it will not last for very long at all.

Another great example of the game: me. Recently, I had interest in a girl I had met a few times through a friend. She was super cute and fun to be around. There was flirting between us, but then again, I always have some element of flirting when I go out. And I could tell she did too. That's fine though, it was fun!

Until the next time I hung out with her. Long story short, out of nowhere we began making out. As a male, I had to fight my first thoughts on this girl because I actually liked her. In fact, I thought she was almost perfect (keeping in mind I barely knew her). After a night of kissing while our mutual friend wasn't looking (that was a lot of fun) I was left with a major crush. A crush? I am 30 years old and I have a crush? I was shocked.

Then, a few weeks later I decided to throw out my bait and ask my friend what her situation was. Couple things: First, it turns out my friend wasn't nearly as oblivious as I thought. She immediately knew who I was talking about when I told her I had a bit of a crush on someone. You women know far too much, FYI. Second, our mutual friend promptly told me that the girl I was interested in was back with her ex boyfriend.

Hmm.

Well, that sucks.

Would I have liked to see her again and see where the two of us would have ended up? Absolutely. Should I be deflated and think that after making out with me for a night she went back to her ex-boyfriend? I'd be lying if I didn't admit I thought that... but... I don't know what her snapshot is. So, no, I should not think that at all. It has nothing to do with me and I wish her well. And when that doesn't work out for her, I will be here for another make out session.

The point is, I put myself out there and gave it a good ole fashion try. This wasn't the girl I should be dating at this time, but so what? It doesn't mean either her or I are bad people. It means that I got back in the game and I tossed up a hail-mary into the end zone. Unfortunately, an ex-boyfriend safety intercepted my pass attempt. I am sure he scored too. Plus, the extra point. And I am no longer talking about football here. But again, I digress.

What am I going to do about now? I'm going to walk to the sideline, take a sip of water (or another beverage) and get back in the game. I am going to try again because I am smart enough to realize that we aren't compatible at this time. That is all it is. Circumstances. And even if she were single and she decided to run a different route, making my hail-mary pass fall on the ground and bounce all over the place like a fish out of water, then that's okay too.

We have to get back in the game. We have to learn that if we fail, we get back up and dust ourselves off, then try again. I know it's difficult, but if you have been paying attention, then hopefully it is getting easier for you. We need to have our self-confidence back. We need to know that although we are flawed, we are who we are for a reason. And one day, assuming you get back in the game, you will meet someone who will appreciate you for who you are. Flaws and all. In the meantime, have some fun!

Chapter 9

Let Me In!

Well, you did it. You got back in the game. You threw a pass down field and the heavily guarded receiver jumped up and caught that perfectly thrown spiral of pigskin. You, as quarterback, immediately ran to the receiver and both of you jumped up hitting each other's sides in the air. Then you patted their butt and walked off the field together.

Ok, maybe the last part was a bit exaggerated, but you get my drift. Now you have found someone you like and want to keep dating. Or maybe you haven't yet and you're still looking. Either way, our work is far from over. There is one more crucial part that I need to mention before we conclude this journey we have undertook together. As with everything we have discussed, this seems obvious and easy, but it is far from it.

We, as human beings, have a tendency to hold onto our pain, even after we convince ourselves we have let it go. We may have let the past pain go, but many times, it still handicaps the future before us. What I mean by that is simple. We look at our new dating partner and all we can think about is, "Will they be like everyone else and hurt me like the others did?" I have two short answers to that.

First, if you are thinking this, I want to say that it's okay to wonder and be cautious. It's perfectly natural to be anxious over a new relationship or even while thinking about one. Yet, there is still some work to do on your end. Chances are, and I could be wrong here (but probably not), that your new partner has not shown any signs of previous behavior that has hurt you before. Maybe they have, and if so, that is a different story. Most likely, however, they haven't. And you are simply afraid.

You're afraid that because someone else has hurt you, that the same thing will happen again. That is completely understandable. However, it is also unrealistic. How many times have we said that everyone is different? Everyone is unique and we all have different strengths and weaknesses that we bring to the table. Your new partner is not, I repeat, not the same person who hurt you. Do not treat them as such.

While we are at it, let's go a step further. You are not the same person you once were either. You have grown and learned since the last time you were in a relationship. Even if you made the same mistakes repeatedly in past relationships, you are not necessarily destined to repeat them. If you have dealt with the true cause of why you made those mistakes, then you are different. You are not the same person you were in the past relationship that failed you.

What happened in the past between you and your ex, happened in the past between you and your ex. Yes, I just repeated myself repeated myself. Back then; whether it was last week or two years ago, you were a different person way back then. That situation was different, under different circumstances. I dare say that even if you and your ex got back together, the situational dynamics would be different, and therefore the experience would be different in at least a slight manner. Point being, the exact situation will never happen again. It is up to you, from your point of view, to make sure that you do everything in your power so that something similar will not happen again.

A quick example. Of who? Me. Obviously.

Recently I dated this girl for the third time in less than a year. Yeah, you heard me. Three separate times in a year. The first time we dated, things were pretty good but she drifted away. Truthfully, we were both dating other people and I believe (but never asked her) that she chose to date someone else.

The second time we dated was much shorter. She basically called (and by called, I mean text) me and said she had a dream about me and hoped I was well. She said she thought about me from time to time. Of course, this led to meeting for a happy hour. Within a couple of drinks she was kissing me. It felt nice, except for all of the people staring at us. It was familiar and yet a little different. Things had obviously changed in her life.

Sadly, she began to pull away and I said forget it.

Lastly, the third and final time we dated. This was maybe 5 or 6 months after the second time of dating. I sent her a text to see how she was. We met up and took it pretty slow. We ended up dating for a few months and for the most part, it was good. We discussed a future together and I really thought it could work.

Short version of why it didn't work? Well, when life throws you problems, you truly see who people are when you watch them handle those problems. I wasn't impressed. Not to say she is a bad human being. It's just that her style of relating, especially during tense times, was not syncing up with me.

The point of that little story is that I dated the same girl three different times in less than a year. Or did I? I would say that each time we dated, we brought with us more and more experiences that changed how we interacted with one another. The first two times, neither one of us were ready for a true relationship with each other. The third and final time, we were. It didn't work out, but that is what brings me to my second point.

Secondly, when we put ourselves out there to meet and date people, we need to be prepared for the possibility that we crash and burn. We may open ourselves up and allow someone to come in and setup camp inside our hearts, and they may end up burning the whole place to the ground.

We are taking a major risk here by entering the dating game again.

Are you ready for that? Are you capable of experiencing more hurt and pain if that should happen to you? Before you answer, I want to do a quick recap of what we have discussed thus far.

Recall that we cannot control what people do or say to us. We can only control how we react to those things. We know, and understand, that if someone wrongs us, it is not because of who we are, but because that person has a problem within them, which they will need to evaluate at some point. We might be able to assist them in that, but we will never be able to take control and fix it for them. Nor is it our responsibility to belittle them and hound them into submission. This never works; especially for a man.

This means, that no matter how hard we try, we may end up hurt. However, if we understand that the only thing we have control of is ourselves, then we should be able to allow others the opportunity to do, act, or say, whatever they end up doing, acting, or saying. Why? Because we know we will ultimately control how we react to it.

As I said before, it is our choice to decide to deal with it and assist them on their personal journey or to walk away. There is no better example of this than… you guessed it… me.

As I have shared, I was terrified after my divorce. Petrified is more like it. Like Medusa had stared into my eyes and froze me as my eyes and mouth were wide open with fear. Slowly, however, I began to let people back in. Finally, I decided I was ready to date.

After a few failed attempts at dating, I realized something. I was phoning in my performance. I wasn't really trying. I was masquerading at a ball pretending I was. So, I decided to give it a real go.

There was one girl who I thought could help me bring it all together. She was one of my best friends. I knew she had more than friendly feelings for me. And to be honest, I was shocked that she stuck around watching my shenanigans weekend to weekend. Later, she would tell me I was an ass all those weekends she came around and we weren't together and that I hurt her a lot. (Obviously, I never meant to do that, but alas - I digress.)

I chose this woman; let us call her Diane, because Diane knew my story. She knew I was a mess and yet, she stuck around. Diane was there for me. So, one day I sat her down. I cooked her my signature dinner (baked chicken and rice… don't get too excited ladies, although it is delicious) and had a sincere discussion with her about my worries. I told her that I was interested in her for sure and was certainly attracted to her. However, my concern was that I needed her more as a friend than as a lover. I can't recall if she said this or I thought it, but all I remember was an epiphany of, "Why can't she be both?"

Right then and there, we decided that we were officially dating. We were going to do it right and we were in this together. She told me that we would always be friends and that it was worth trying. She said we would regret it if we didn't. Don't tell her this... but she was right on all accounts.

So what happened, you ask? Well, it was great. For a while. She, to this day, is the most amazing person I have ever met. I talked to her all day every day for months. Am I exaggerating? No. Not one bit, actually. We were best friends. We were lovers. It was amazing. I hadn't felt those feelings since before I was even married. And yes, you read that right. I loved her and I told her that. I meant it.

Unfortunately, love was not enough. Remember the good ole line, "It's not you, it's me?" I used that line. Except this time, the person who said it truly meant it. Everything I just said to you was true. She is perfect. Me? Not even close. And I knew it. As we began to go down the winding relationship trail, I went through all of the chapters before this one. My last chapter in my current love story... is this one.

In simple terms, I wouldn't let her in. To my credit, I truly believed I did. I was working hard at it. I really was! I finally came to the realization that something was holding me back. I had to take a minute and search for what that was. Luckily for me, but sadly for our relationship, I found it.

I had not yet closed the final chapter in the book with my ex-wife. I was still tied to her. I was not in love with her or had those romantic feelings for her, but my heart was still invested in her. My heart and soul was not completely mine to give to someone. If my entire heart wasn't mine to begin with, how could I truly give it to another?

Had this girl been a bimbo or something, perhaps I would have had my fun and went on my merry way. But, no. Diane was special. She didn't deserve this kind of treatment from me. So, I let her go. I told her that I had unresolved issues and it was going to take time for me to be what she wanted me to be. What she deserved.

She never pushed me into a corner or pressured me. She never told me I was dumb or that what I was trying to do was unreasonable. She only begged to help me. She pleaded for me to reconsider my stance that I had to do this alone. Ultimately, I broke her heart. I lost my lover. I lost my best friend. I felt like I lost everything. And what's worse, is that I had caused all of the heartache between us.

The aftermath left me feeling as if I was an asshole. I was the one who did this (technically, that part was true). I told my friend how upset I was and that I was heartbroken as well. Their response? "What about Diane? How do you think she is feeling?" That only made me feel worse. I was lost.

That brought me back here, to this magnificent book. I realized that I wasn't done with my journey. Interestingly enough, I had stopped on this very chapter many months ago. I called it writers block, but I now see that I wasn't ready to write about this just yet. Now, having experienced this very issue, I was finally ready to write.

Where did I go wrong? Easy... I didn't let Diane inside my heart and soul. I said that I had and I truly believed that I had. But if I look at the situation honestly, I hadn't. Even after she pleaded and plainly pointed out my mistakes as they were happening, I still didn't let her in. She was doing that with love, not contempt. I knew that, even while it was happening. It wasn't her. It was me.

However, my stance here is that I was not in the wrong in my decision. I wasn't ready. I wasn't prepared to let Diane in just yet. That was no reflection on her as person, or as my girlfriend. It also didn't make me a bad person. This is simply my snapshot in time and where I am. I have more work to do before I can truly give myself to another person.

Just as I took a chance, you will one day need to take a chance. You need to be prepared for more heartache in case that happens. I certainly experienced my fair share with Diane and I know I caused her more than her fair share of pain. However, this is the final step in our journey of self-repair. If we have performed the steps outlined above in the previous chapters, then we should be ready.

Are you ready? Are you ready to take that chance? You may crash and burn or you may live happily ever after.

If you aren't ready… join the club. I am the President of that club. And that's okay! Again, it doesn't make us bad people. We simply need more work before we can let people, even the best of the best such as Diane, into our hearts and into our worlds. Eventually, we will have to let them in otherwise, we run the risk of no one wanting to deal with us. It is time to take a chance and let them in.

Chapter 10

Conclusion

Well, that was fun. Wasn't it? While writing this, I learned a lot about myself and I hope you learned about yourself as well. If nothing else, you were privileged enough to hear more than you wanted to know about this authors love life and my monumental screw ups. Truth be told, I wouldn't take (most) of those screw-ups back if I could.

Why?

As I have shared in the pages leading up to this conclusion, we are who we are based on our life choices and experiences. Each failed relationship has taught me something. Some of them have been HUGE lessons, such as never date sisters... it doesn't turn out well. Other lessons have been small; such as always clean up your tiny whiskers after shaving. In fact, let me go ahead and name some lessons I learned along the way. Most are for men, but there are a few for you women out there as well. Hopefully, someone can learn from my mistakes.

Some hard truths:

1. Always keep a clean kitchen. This is not the exclusive job of women.

2. Never do a woman's laundry without talking to her first.
3. And even then, don't do it. If you shrink something... God help you.
4. Men, put the toilet seat down. I mean, c'mon.
5. Never call a woman angry or tell her to calm down, even when she is angry and needs to calm down.
6. "No, those jeans do NOT make you look fat," is the only acceptable answer.
7. Men, when you are asked number 6, don't look at her longer than .4 seconds before you answer. But always pretend to look at what she is wearing.
8. Don't say you're sorry unless you mean it (women can tell the difference).
9. Never forget a birthday.
10. Never forget an anniversary.
11. Women – us men really hate Valentine's Day.
12. Forget her screw-ups.
13. Never forget YOUR screw-ups (she won't).
14. Unless she asks, kitchen appliances are not an acceptable gift for any occasion. Period.
15. "Yes, dinner was great," is the only correct answer after she cooks you dinner.
16. Some things are not worth fighting about, such as her bathroom counter space.
17. Men, your girlfriend/wife is not your mother.

18. Ladies, your boyfriend/husband is not your daddy (insert jokes here).
19. Do not underestimate a healthy sex life.
20. Do not overestimate how much of your sex life overshadows other parts of your relationship. Sex is only a slice of the relationship pie.
21. During the fall, Saturdays and Sundays are reserved for Football. Sorry ladies.
22. Men, if your woman is kind enough to give you Saturdays and Sundays for football, make it up to her in other ways. And sex rarely counts here.
23. Men, many times making your woman watch sports is like her making you watch three back-to-back episodes of Sex and the City. It's brutal.
24. Men, when asked a question and you answer "yes" or "no," at the very least, look up to see if that answer satisfied your significant other. Chances are - that answer is not good enough. Life is in the details.
25. During Guys Night Out, send her a sweet text while your boys are not looking.
26. Do NOT expect her to do the same thing during Girls Night Out.
27. If, your woman asks if a girl is prettier than her, the answer is always "no."
28. However, if your woman asks if a girl is pretty, do NOT lie. If she is pretty, say "yes," then immediately

tell your woman she is prettier. Lying here will do you no good. They can tell.

29. Never tell a woman what she is thinking, feeling, or what she wants. Only she knows that. And sometimes, she doesn't even know.

30. Men - you are wrong 99% of the time.

31. Men - the 1% you are actually right, ask yourself if it's worth arguing over.

32. Men - it's never worth arguing over.

33. Never, under any circumstances, mention the letters PMS.

34. Seriously, don't do it guys.

35. Never let your friends pick on your woman. At least not in front of her.

36. Never lie.

37. If you have to delete a text after you send it so your significant other will not see it... you probably shouldn't have sent it.

38. Guys, your ability to have 30 head shots in a row on a video game is NOT sexy.

39. Women crave love and attention.

40. Men crave respect. (And sex.)

41. None of us is owed anything. Everything is a privilege that must be earned.

42. If you ask for it, and receive it, don't be mad about it.

43. If someone has not broken your trust, then they deserve to be trusted.

44. If a woman does not want to talk to you at a bar, repeatedly asking "why not" is NOT going to change her mind. Also see number 5.

45. Guys, a girls core group of friends approval is almost more important than your girls approval.

46. Guys, don't stare at women when you're out with your girlfriend/wife. This gives her a complex and trust me - you WILL deal with the aftereffects.

47. If your girlfriend or wife asks if she should bring a jacket, the answer is yes. And realize you will be holding it for her.

48. If, at the movies, your girlfriend is indecisive about getting popcorn, go ahead and get it. Otherwise, you will miss the previews or the first 10 minutes of the movie.

49. Men, know and understand that the obscene amount of money that your significant other spends on things such as make-up, clothes, hair products, etc., is actually for you. Just let it be.

50. Number 49 does not give you the right to go buy a 55-inch TV on a whim.

51. Always open the door for her.

52. Say thank you when she does nice things for you. This includes things that you THINK you expect from her.

53. Except after sex, that would just be weird.

54. If you are married, you married each other's families. Yes, that usually sucks, but get over it. It was your choice.

55. Men, unless a woman starts or finishes a sentence with "What should I do?" she is not asking you to solve her problems. She just wants you to listen.

56. Men, actually listen and not just during commercials.

57. Guys, learn to like chick flicks. They aren't that bad.

58. Guys, learn to convince yourself of things to better your relationship (number 57).

59. The movie Die Hard is not the kind of Christmas movie she has in mind.

60. The last bite is always hers.

61. So is the first bite.

62. Actually, any bite in between is hers too. Just be glad you get to eat.

63. If you introduce your woman to friends but haven't had "the conversation" yet, just say, "This is _____." Do not call her your friend, unless you want to keep it that way.

64. Sharing an appetizer is not foreplay.

65. Guys, most girls do not follow the 3-date rule. It can range anywhere from the first date to the night of your marriage. It's her choice, not yours.
66. Women, in case you forgot, you have the power.
67. Ladies, sleeping on the couch is not really a punishment. It's kind of an adventure for us and makes us feel like we are in college again.
68. "Are you wearing that shirt?" is not cool. Find a better way to say it, please.
69. Men, figure this number out. It's important to her.
70. Always lift each other up to your friends and family. Even when your significant other isn't around.
71. Men, hold her hand.
72. Ladies, hold his arm.
73. Be adventurous together. Your Guys/Girls Night Out should include a story like… "Dudes, you'll never guess where the wife and I snuck into to have sex the other night."
74. Help each other.
75. Ladies, if we are building something, such as an entertainment center, we are actually doing our best to be manly in front of you. Even if we look ridiculous and mess it up, give us some credit.
76. Men, do not wait until Christmas Eve to get her a gift.
77. Ladies, buying you presents is extremely stressful.
78. Men, a gift card to Victoria Secret is not a sexy gift.

79. Ladies, buying us men a gift card to Victoria Secret and asking us to come with you and pick something out IS a sexy gift.

80. Ladies, we can be manipulated very easily, without even knowing it. Example: number 79. We would think you were being all sexy, when all you really did was basically buy yourself lingerie, which you were planning on buying anyway.

81. Texts, emails, Facebook posts are cute, but they are not a replacement for human contact. Especially during special occasions such as Birthdays.

82. Guys, women will be "running late" constantly.

83. Once you live with her, you realize she has NO excuse for always running late. Keep this to yourself.

84. If you are unable to keep number 83 to yourself, it is never okay to leave her because she isn't dressed yet, even when she tells you it's okay.

85. If a woman says she is "fine," she isn't.

86. If you ask to break plans with her to hang out with your buddies and she says that its "up to you," then do not go. Ever.

87. Guys, if you are like me, you hate buying roses on Valentine's Day. This is not an excuse to NEVER buy her flowers.

88. The smallest gestures, such as surprising her with a cup of coffee in the morning, will do wonders.

89. Men, your penis is not magic. Every guy has one and most women prefer the plastic kind anyway.
90. Ladies, we are fascinated with your lady parts because we do not have them. Please excuse our groping.
91. Ladies, us men are stupid. If we forget something important, it usually isn't because we are being hateful or vindictive. We literally are that dumb sometimes.
92. Pick your battles in all areas of life. Trade the color of the bedroom walls for the sofa you really like.
93. Compromising will make you happy.
94. Compromising is impossible without open and honest communication.
95. Healthy conflict is good.
96. Different opinions are what make us unique. Those opinions are typically what intrigued us about you in the first place. Never forget that.
97. Never, under any circumstance, say I love you if you don't mean it.
98. If you do mean it, say I love you all the time.
99. Never, ever, allow your significant other to ever wonder how you feel.

Before we complete our journey and relationship as author and reader, I have one last thing to share. As I drew nearer to the end of my journey of self-discovery, I wrote another poem. I was ready to start new. I had already taken a few steps to start a new life, but I realized I skipped a lot of steps along the way. I went back, fixed what I needed to, and ended up ready to face the challenges of tomorrow.

The following poem is entitled, Today. In it, I addressed all of my exes that I felt had hurt me along the way. I hope you enjoy.

'Today' can be my new beginning
To fly free on an outstretched wing
A chance to transform into who I want to be
When the time comes, I must stand firm and not flee

We decide our own path and our own fate
Sadly, most people learn this fact way too late
Deep inside, everyone has the strength to amend
They spent most of their lives in a state of pretend

Moving forward my eyes focus straight ahead
One day, I will find someone better to be in your stead
I smile at the past, but leave you far behind
I will find someone loving, thoughtful and kind

Thank you for the memories and the tears
You no longer have control of my hopes and my fears
I emerged bloody, bruised, black and blue
Now that you're gone, I see my only limitation was you

So today is the day I blaze my own trail
I will certainly stumble and may even fail
I refuse to counterfeit myself just for you
Without you, I am positive I will pull through

Today I start my life anew

I am over you, yes it's true
I feel bad for your next prey
But I no longer care, today is my brand new day

Finally, that is enough about me (I know you are saying "finally, you self-absorbed jerk"). It is my sincere desire that you have enjoyed this little endeavor between us. If you are like me, your snapshot in time is somewhere between the first page and the last. As I just shared, I am somewhere between getting back in the game and truly opening up. It will take time for me, as it will take time for you.

Most importantly, we need to realize we are in control. We own our own destiny and we have the power to choose. We can choose to get through our past and make the right choices in relationships. We have the ability to learn and grow. We need to realize that the dating world is truly jacked up, yet, we can make it better. We can be that fresh air in the douchiness of dating. We have that power.

I say it is our time. It is time we suck it up, suck it in and get back out there. Play hard and fast (insert joke here). Be truthful, to a fault. Know when to speak and when to listen (if in doubt, always listen). Learn when to make your move and when to sit on the sidelines. Trial and error should be your friend, not your feared enemy. Take every failure as a learning opportunity, not a reason to feel sorry for yourself.

Live life, people! Love it! Embrace it! Manhandle it! Just get out there and enjoy yourself. Most of us have lost someone special to old age, perhaps an elderly family member. I can guarantee that on their deathbeds they were not laying there thinking of all the people that hurt them throughout the years. They were thinking of those who they loved and who loved them. I can also imagine they thought of all the things they wish they would have done or could have done different.

Do not end up like that. Have no regrets. Forgive those who wronged you. Forgive yourself. Love others and allow them to love you in return. When we look back, we will see a life full of happiness and we can smile knowing that there was a point in time we made a choice. A choice to forget the past and look to the future.

For me, that choice is here. That time is now. I am ready to make my choice and start my brand new day. Are you?

Thank you to everyone who supported me during this process. Healing a broken heart is not a quick and easy task. The love and support from my family and friends brought me out of darkness and back to the light. You will never know how grateful I am to each of you who played a part in saving my life.

Sincerely,

C. L. Bartley

www.ingramcontent.com/pod-product-compliance
Lightning Source LLC
Chambersburg PA
CBHW022123280326
41933CB00007B/524